The Jesus Way

STUDY GUIDE

D1611601

The Jesus Way

STUDY GUIDE

Eugene H. Peterson and Peter Santucci

WILLIAM B. EERDMANS PUBLISHING COMPANY
GRAND RAPIDS, MICHIGAN / CAMBRIDGE, U.K.

© 2007 Eugene H. Peterson and Peter Santucci
All rights reserved

Published 2007 by
Wm. B. Eerdmans Publishing Co.
2140 Oak Industrial Drive N.E., Grand Rapids, Michigan 49505 /
P.O. Box 163, Cambridge CB3 9PU U.K.
www.eerdmans.com

Printed in the United States of America

12 11 10   7 6 5 4 3 2

Library of Congress Cataloging-in-Publication Data

Peterson, Eugene H., 1932-
The Jesus way study guide / Eugene H. Peterson and Peter Santucci.
p.   cm.
ISBN 978-0-8028-4566-5 (pbk.: alk. paper)
1. Jesus Christ — Example — Textbooks.   2. Christian life — Textbooks.
3. Christianity and culture — Textbooks.   4. Apologetics — Textbooks.
5. Bible — Criticism, interpretation, etc. — Textbooks.
I. Santucci, Peter.   II. Title.

BT304.2.P482   2007
232 — dc22

2007014186

The Jesus Way is published in association with the literary agency of Alive Com-
munications, Inc., 7680 Goddard Street #200, Colorado Springs, CO 80290

Contents

CONTENTS

Contents

CONTENTS

Preface

It's all about adjectives. Adjectives bend nouns and move them in different directions, just like adverbs bend verbs. A good adjective can send a noun in a wonderful, growing, expansive direction. But a bad adjective can kill it. Consider the noun "genius." Someone can be a creative genius or an evil genius. Same noun; two drastically different realities. The adjectives are what divide heroes from villains.

Eugene Peterson has been working to rehabilitate Christian nouns throughout his book-writing career by giving intense attention and scrutiny to the adjectives we use with those nouns. In doing so, Peterson provides one of the most important services to the Christian church. Because even though most Christians in most places and times have agreed on the What of following Jesus, where we've erred and fallen into the ditch is in the How. What is the realm of nouns, but How is the realm of adjectives.

The Jesus Way is a book about adjectives and restoring a biblical imagination when following Jesus. No matter which culture the church has found itself in, it has had its biblical adjectives stolen from it and replaced by the adjectives of the surrounding culture. With the same intensity and attention to the biblical accounts that he has shown elsewhere, Peterson goes to the heart of what it means to be a follower of Jesus in this book, restoring our biblically conditioned adjectives to us.

The chapters of *The Jesus Way* deal with topics familiar to Christians who read books like *The Purpose Driven Life* and other how-to Christian books, but they always surprise and always raise new sets of questions.

For instance: Recently I was with four other Presbyterian pastors, preparing to lead our elders on a retreat. I asked them what adjectives they would use with the noun "worship." The answers included "passionate," "intimate," "relational," "authentic," and a few other words that get tossed around in popular books and articles about worship. But when I flipped to Chapter Five in *The Jesus Way*, where Peterson describes Elijah's influence on worship, it was the adjective "prophetic" that came to the surface. In other words, more than anything else, worship challenges our idolatries by placing God in front of us. When the adjective "passionate" describes our worship, who is worship really all about? Us. Because what determines if it's real worship is our passion or lack of it. But if worship is "prophetic," what determines if it's real is the proclamation of God and his character in a world of false gods.

Now I have to admit that I don't always agree with Peterson's choice of adjectives. But agreement isn't Peterson's goal. That's why this book is subtitled "a conversation," not "a monologue." Peterson's intent is not so much to replace the adjectives popularly used with ones that he's suggesting (though I'm sure he'd consider that an improvement in many cases). Rather, his intent is to shake us out of receiving without question the adjectives that have been handed to us. Again, Christians throughout time have agreed on the nouns. It's the adjectives that need some serious work.

Peterson gets at this when he talks about means and ends. "Setting the goal requires little effort, no commitment, and no skill. But finding the means for reaching the goal, achieving that identity, is a matter of diligent concentration, responsible perseverance, and keen discernment" (p. 27).

To keep our adjectives in line, Peterson insists on two things: Scripture and prayer.

First, only Scripture can shape the way. So the first section of *The Jesus Way* shows us how Scripture can shape our adjectives by looking at the largest characters of the Bible that Jesus himself read, what we call the Old Testament. (These, of course, aren't the only sources in Scripture to shape our imaginations as we travel the Jesus way. Make an effort to search all of the Bible for other sources. Continue the conversation that Peterson is starting.)

Second, only prayer can keep us from drifting into other ways. A biblical imagination isn't enough. We need continual connection with the God of the Bible to keep us in the way. And we need praying companions. So in the second section of the book, Peterson gives us some representative praying companions in Mary, Thomas, and the early Christian community to give us an idea of how praying (and specifically, praying in community) can keep us from wandering from the Jesus way into the myriad other ways that are continually being offered to us. (Ideally, you're reading and reflecting on this book within a praying community.)

You can use the tool of this study guide on your own and gain from it, but it is best used in a community of Christians. There's a certain level of honesty that can be reached only when questions are answered aloud in front of people who know us, and honest speech becomes a truth event in which we articulate things that we may not have intended to say but that change us as a result. Silent thoughts that don't escape the mind rarely do that.

This study guide is currently formatted for an 11-session study, with the introduction and each chapter receiving its own attention. Each session begins with Peterson's main chapter title followed by my own "fleshing out" subtitle of sorts. I thought this would be a good way to encapsulate the primary truth Peterson is telling in that chapter. Each session also features a chapter summary. I've included this for the sake of the group leader(s). You may or may not want to read this aloud before the group discussion. One problem with reading summaries aloud in small groups is that such summaries can lead to laziness, as when I was in eighth grade and read CliffNotes on *Moby Dick* instead of the complete novel.

Following each summary, I've included a brief section called "Key Adjectives," which highlight the adjectives Peterson has used to describe key figures he's discussing. The range of adjectives is always surprising and stimulating. These in and of themselves could prompt illuminating discussion.

Along with questions for interaction, I've included quotations to consider. Peterson is eminently quotable, and I've had to restrain myself with the number of quotations included. At times we need questions to spark our interaction, but at other times, simply reading a powerful and representative quotation is more effective in generating interaction.

But remember, this guide includes a lot of quotations and questions. Make sure you consider the amount of time you have available for conversation and discussion before you pick which ones to use. Simply starting with the first question or the first quotation and trying to get through them all would be a mistake, unless you're using this guide for personal study. No group I know could have any depth of interaction while dealing with all the quotations and questions.

I've also ended each session with a prayer. I've called these sections "Praying with Traveling Companions on the Jesus Way" because I've featured prayers from a range of believers over the span of centuries.

If you're using this study guide with a group that's been meeting together for a while, you probably have an established rhythm and way of interacting. If you're fairly new at this or are willing to explore a different shape for your time together, here's how our community groups operate (the groups I had in mind when I wrote this guide). It's fairly simple. We gather for a meal. The sharing of food makes it much easier to share our lives. Church-related talk isn't permitted during meals. Talk about anything and everything else is encouraged. After the meal, we have our discussion time. Next, we take a break for dessert. And then we gather again for prayer. That's all. It's not a foolproof technique, but it's a basic rhythm that makes sure that not only are we discussing the passage or book for that evening, but we're also engaging each other as friends and praying for each other.

Whatever shape your group takes, make sure to take time to pray together, bringing before God your daily experiences and your engagement with Scripture. Hopefully, the conversations coming out of your discussions of the questions and quotations in this guide will give you plenty to pray over.

And speaking of conversations, I would like to thank my most constant conversation partners: my family. My wife, Charlene, and our four children — Emett, Lydia Grace, Josiah, and Matthias (who calls himself "Bono") — keep my adjectives honest. They keep me personal, relational, and real in the dailiness of life together. More than anyone else, they keep my life grateful and prayerful.

I finished this manuscript — which I hope will help stimulate many productive conversations — at The Lebanon Coffee Company. For the espresso and tea, thanks! *The Crane Wife* by The Decemberists provided a wonderfully storied musical backdrop.

Lent 2007   PETER SANTUCCI

Introduction: "The Purification of Means"; or, The Countercultural Way of Biblical Adjectives

(pp. 1-18)

Summary

It's possible to claim the name Christian without being Christian at all — that is, without following Christ. Jesus is far more than a theological icon to believe in; he is a person to follow. He is not just the truth; he is the way.

But those who follow Jesus are constantly in danger of getting lost, for we live in a culture that stands in huge contrast to Jesus. The American way is not the Jesus way. It is based on consumption, which is fueled by insatiable appetites and want-more acquisition.

Our culture is functional, reducing people to machine-like doers of things. But, as Peterson reminds us, "the gospel is personal or it is nothing."

Jesus shows us how to live this gospel-based life, but he doesn't give us a how-to manual. Rather, the local congregation, the company of praying men and women, is the primary place where we discover the way of Jesus. The church's worship and mission are done in community. However, this insistently local and personal community is endangered by American methods, which reduce relationships to functions.

We need different ways, different methods. We need a new set of adjectives to shape the way we follow the way of Jesus. We need to go the countercultural way of biblical adjectives.

SESSION 1

Key Adjectives

Personal, embodied, incarnate, relational, particular, local, named, recognizable, familiar, interrelational, dynamic, holy, Trinitarian, comprehensive, biblical, historical, liturgical, righteous, eternal, ordinary, incisive, vigilant, active, urgent, worshiping, evangelizing, witnessing, reconciling, peace-making, justice-advocating, clear, definitive, invisible, triumphant, integrated, practiced, immediate, communal, intimate, praying, sacrificial, Eucharistic, God-fearing, God-worshiping, organic, intricate, patient, embracing, serious, deep, re-imagined, re-configured, re-oriented, obedient, imaginative, radical, different, daily, discerning, discriminating, distinctive, dignified, vigorous, bold, non-expert, baptismal, active, responsible, free, rescued, beleaguered, scriptural, priestly, mutual, wide-ranging, historical, theological, unique, countercultural, impervious, conversational, saved

Quotations to Consider

"The ways Jesus goes about loving and saving the world are personal: nothing disembodied, nothing abstract, nothing impersonal" (p. 1).

"Jesus is an alternative to the dominant ways of the world, not a supplement to them" (p. 2).

"If any of the *means* we use to follow Jesus are extraneous to who we are in Jesus — detached "things" or role "models" — they detract from the *end* of following Jesus" (p. 2).

"The Jesus way wedded to the Jesus truth brings about the Jesus life" (p. 4).

"We can't proclaim the Jesus truth but then do it any old way we like. Nor can we follow the Jesus way without speaking the Jesus truth" (p. 4).

"Jesus as the truth gets far more attention that Jesus as the way" (p. 4).

"We cannot skip the way of Jesus in our hurry to get the truth of Jesus as he is worshiped and proclaimed. The way of Jesus is the way that we prac-

2

tice and come to understand the truth of Jesus, living Jesus in our homes and workplaces, with our friends and family" (p. 4).

"The great American innovation in congregation is to turn it into a consumer enterprise" (p. 6).

Questions for Interaction

1. In what ways do you experience our culture as impersonal as opposed to personal? In what ways have Christians followed suit?
2. In what ways does Christian "culture" mirror American culture?
3. In what ways has consumerism affected the church? For instance, have you ever gone "shopping" for a church?
4. What adjectives would the average person on the street use to describe Christians?
5. What adjectives would you use to describe your church? Yourself?
6. What adjectives would you expect Jesus to use to describe his followers?

Praying with traveling companions on the Jesus way: John Calvin (1509-1564)

Grant, almighty God, that as you shine on us by your Word, we may not be blind at midday, nor willfully seek darkness, and thus lull our minds asleep: but, may we be roused daily by your words, and may we stir up ourselves more and more to fear your name and thus present ourselves and all our pursuits as a sacrifice to you, that you may peaceably rule and perpetually dwell in us, until you gather us to your celestial habitation, where there is reserved for us eternal rest and glory, through Jesus Christ our Lord. Amen.

PART I

The Way of Jesus

Jesus: "I Am the Way . . .";
or, The Relational Way of Obediently Following Jesus

(pp. 21-41)

Summary

Repent, believe, and follow — the imperatives that Jesus presents us with — are matched by who Jesus is as Way, Truth, and Life. Just as we discover the truth as we believe in Jesus and discover life as we follow him, we find our way as we repent of following our own ways and turn to follow Jesus in his way. But that way isn't a literal road or path; it is a method, a how-we-do-things way. Jesus isn't just a who or a what; he's a how. As Peterson notes, "the way we go on the way" is just as important as going on the way in the first place.

Getting in on this Jesus way first of all requires attentiveness. What is God doing, and how is he doing it? The second thing that is required is responsiveness. This way calls for participation. We see, we hear, we walk. How do we get in on what God is doing?

The word "way" is, of course, a metaphor. Jesus isn't a road, at least not literally. From the very moment we set foot on the "way," we are required to use our imaginations. And the use of imagination requires participation.

Metaphor helps us deal with God because there is no other kind of language that is suited for transcendence. Metaphor shows the links between the visible and the invisible. Everyday, nonreligious words become windows into holy realities. As Peterson puts it, "When used as a metaphor, a word explodes, comes alive — it starts *moving*" (p. 26).

Metaphors are more necessary now than ever. The technological mind has taken over our language and, as a result, the way we think and go about doing things. "Technology has a monopoly, at least in the minds of most, on answering questions regarding means" (p. 27).

After Jesus is baptized into the kingdom-of-heaven way, he "immediately" heads into the wilderness to be tempted. The temptations in the desert show the basic divide between the Jesus way and the devil way.

We never have just one option, one way laid out before us. Along with the Jesus way, there are the devil's ways — and they are plentiful — to choose against. The devil's ways are always tempting and always illusory. The devil doesn't worry about the ends. If he can trip us up in the means, the way, we'll never get to the end.

According to Peterson, the devil tempts us in ways reminiscent of his challenges of Jesus. Jesus' first temptation is to turn stones into bread, to do something useful. Similarly, we are tempted to use Jesus to fulfill needs instead of following him, "to deal with myself and others first as and foremost as consumers" (p. 31). This reduces life to needs to be filled and problems to be solved.

Jesus' second temptation is to jump off the temple roof, to dazzle the people below with a miracle. Similarly, we are tempted to use Jesus for entertainment instead of following him, which turns us from participants into spectators. We need to remember that Jesus does not lead us into escapism but plunges us into the depths of the dailiness of life.

Jesus' third temptation is to rule the world. Similarly, we are tempted to use Jesus to control our worlds instead of following him, trading personal interaction for abstract authority.

Peterson reminds us that "we cannot do the Lord's work in the devil's ways" (p. 36). There is only one way: "Jesus is the way we come to God. Period. End of discussion" (p. 37). Not only is Jesus the vehicle by which we come to God; he is also the road on which that vehicle travels. We have a destination, but the territory we cover along the way is just as important. In fact, Peterson says, we need to spend less time focusing on the destination and more time focusing on the journey in all its many facets. Peterson writes, "Too many of my faith-companions for too long have been reducing the way of Jesus simply to the route to heaven, which it certainly is. But there is so much more" (p. 41).

The "much more" of the Jesus way includes all of Scripture. The Jesus story isn't in red-letter isolation from the rest of the Bible. Rather, it gathers into it all of the other stories in Scripture that come before it. In the remaining chapters of the book Peterson will attempt to open up aspects of the Jesus way by looking at several of these other stories, these other ways.

Key Adjectives

metaphorical, participatory, interconnected, comprehensive, obedient, visible, audible, congruent, derivative, brief, punchy, wide, simple, solid, listening, answering, rooted, growing, attentive, responsive, intricate, discerning

Quotations to Consider

"To follow Jesus means that we can't separate what Jesus is saying from what Jesus is doing and the way that he is doing it" (p. 22).

"Metaphor is language that in a single word conveys the indivisibility of visible and invisible, of seen and unseen, of heaven and earth" (p. 25).

"Means have to fit ends. Otherwise everything falls apart" (p. 27).

"A technologized world knows how to make things, knows how to get places, but is not conspicuous for living well" (p. 28).

"There are wrong ways to be on 'the way of the Lord'" (p. 29).

"The devil is content to leave the matter of ends — the goal, the purpose, the grand work of salvation — uncontested. His tempting is devoted exclusively to *ways*, to the means that are best suited to accomplish the end to which Jesus is the way" (p. 30).

"The way of Jesus is not a sequence of exceptions to the ordinary, but a way of living deeply and fully with the people here and now, in the place we find ourselves" (p. 33).

"The rhetoric that we are a Christian nation is not supported by the performance of our political leaders, our business community, or our institutions of learning" (p. 34).

"The devil is the ultimate in disincarnation. Every time that we embrace ways other than the ways of Jesus, try to manipulate people or events in ways that short-circuit personal relationships and intimacies, we are doing the devil's work" (p. 36).

"[Jesus] doesn't point out the way and then step aside and let us get there on our own as best we can. Jesus points out the way, but then he takes the initiative, inviting us to go with him" (p. 36).

"Everything we need to know of God comes by way of Jesus" (p. 38).

"The Way that is Jesus cannot be reduced to information or instruction. The Way is a person whom we believe and follow as God-with-us" (p. 40).

Questions for Interaction

1. The "kingdom of God" is the center of what Jesus proclaimed. What difficulties arise with the word "kingdom"? How is "kingdom" helpful in defining reality in terms of God?
2. "To repent" is to change directions, to give up going one way and start going another way. In what ways might you need to "repent" in order to go in the direction Jesus is going, to follow his way?
3. Metaphors take everyday, nonreligious words and use them to pry open our imaginations, especially in relation to God. What are your favorite biblical metaphors for God? (See the Psalms for numerous examples.) Take a few minutes to try out a few new ones. What feels awkward about making new metaphors? What feels faith-enlivening about it?
4. Share a story of when you've done the right thing but in the wrong way (coercing someone, becoming angry with someone, etc.). Do the means ever justify the ends?
5. In what ways have Christians done the right thing in the wrong way?
6. If technology calls the shots in matters of means, it corrupts what we do. How can technology be used in ways that do not "obscure the vital organic connections between means and ends" (p. 28)?
7. What are some adjectives that describe the ways in which Jesus is the way? What are some adjectives that are *never* used to describe the way Jesus is the way? Are you surprised by any words that are included or excluded? (Feel free to use the Bible!)

8. How much of your life is focused on meeting needs — at home, on the job, at church, and elsewhere? What other important things might you be neglecting in the process?

9. How much "entertainment" do you consume each week? Count not just television but light fiction, magazines, music, soft drinks, and anything else that you consume to "lighten" life. Do they do more than add some spice to life? How does too much entertainment move us from participants in life to spectators of life? In what ways does it distract us from the Jesus way?

10. This phrase (or something like it) is common among church leaders: As long as the message is the same, it doesn't matter how you get it across. In what ways is that true? In what ways do methods actually change the message?

11. How does a focus on heaven as the destination of Christians undermine the day-to-day following of the Jesus way here and now?

Praying with traveling companions on the Jesus way: Sir Richard of Chichester (1198-1253)

O most merciful Redeemer, friend and brother, may we know you more clearly, love you more dearly, and follow you more nearly, for your own sake.

Abraham: Climbing Mount Moriah; or, The Sacrificial Way of Obedient Faith

(pp. 42-58)

Summary

The defining point of the story of Abraham is the binding of Isaac on Mount Moriah. It's a moment of darkness when the goodness of God comes under question. It's offensive to think that a loving God would require the murder of a person's child. But as uncomfortable as it is, the way of Abraham leads us into the way of obedient faith.

Faith connects the visible and the invisible, body and soul, earth and heaven. Faith is living as if there is more than meets the eye. Contrary to popular opinion, faith is not an inner life. It's an obedient life that involves all of who we are, body and soul.

Faith reminds us that this life isn't all about us and that we're not in charge. It moves us away from trying to control what's going on around us and opens us up to seeing and engaging with what God is doing around us.

Abraham is the one who shows us best what the way of faith is like — "not faith as a doctrine to be taught and learned but a certain way of being in the truth that extends beyond reason's ability to fully grasp" (p. 45). All of Scripture looks to Abraham to define the life of faith, a defining that has less to do with definitions as we know them than with stories.

The first verb of the Abraham story and the culminating command of the Jesus story is "Go!" Faith moves us out of a self-oriented world and launches us into what God is doing in the world. Because of that, it is less about duties to perform and prospects to chase than it is about engaging with God, following him, obeying him.

Faith is too involved to be explained or defined. Dictionaries are less helpful than stories, because faith is a kind of complex story: it draws together everything of God and the world and us into a way of life, taking all of the details seriously. It is something that is only true when participated in. Copying someone else ruins it. "We are all originals when we live by faith," Peterson says (p. 48).

But that doesn't make faith easy. On the contrary, faith is a hard road to travel. It is the way of testing and sacrifice, as we are constantly honed, re-oriented, re-adjusted, and rescued from our self-deceit. Abraham lives a life of sacrifice, "each sacrifice an act of discernment, separating the chaff of illusion from the wheat of promise" (pp. 49-50).

Sacrifice requires relinquishment, a letting go, a leaving behind. Each time we relinquish something to God, we travel lighter, cleaner. A life of getting is exchanged for a life of receiving. Self-sovereignty is traded for God-sovereignty.

As painful as it is, the way of faith reveals that "relinquishment is prerequisite to fulfillment, that letting go of a cramped self-will [opens us] up to an expansive God-willed life" (p. 50). Faithful sacrifice turns the whine of loss into the thank you for all that God gives. "Sacrifice is not diminishment. . . . It does not result in less joy, less satisfaction, less fulfillment, but in more" (p. 51).

The way of faith is always the way of sacrifice. Without sacrifice, the journey of faith comes to a standstill. "Sacrifice is to faith what eating is to nutrition" (p. 51).

Because it is so difficult, we need preparation and allies for this way of sacrificial faith. Along the way, because we inevitably become victims of self-delusion and deceit, we need to be tested. And because of our self-delusion, none of us can be trusted to test ourselves. Our self-deception needs to be weeded out.

Testing reveals the difference between a life of awe and worship and obedience (a life that takes God on his terms, serving him) and a life of religious consumption (a life that reduces God to an idol, a god designed to serve us), exposing so-called faith as no-faith. Testing always reveals our desire to control God and returns us to the place where God is God and we are not. And this always comes at a cost, "for we can get very attached to our little projects of self-deification" (pp. 54-55).

13

Moriah wasn't a vacation in the mountains. Rather, it was a time of brutal testing that brought to light a deeper, more complex faith than there had been before. It exposed the sacrificial way of obedient faith that Abraham had been walking for a century.

Key Adjectives

trusting, obedient, relational, venturing, resolute, firm, engaged, deliberate, risky, multi-dimensioned, responsive, open, ready, embracing, passionate, personal, immediate, embraced, followed, participatory, original, sacrificial, relinquishing, lightening, receiving, tested, mature, present, painful

Quotations to Consider

"Faith has to do with marrying Invisible and Visible" (p. 44).

"[Faith] is most certainly not a disposition, an 'inner life.' It is an obedient life, a deliberate engagement of the will, a fusion of body and spirit, visible and invisible fused, taking us somewhere" (p. 44).

"The way of Abraham continues today. . . . Somewhere along the way we realize that we are not in charge of our own lives" (p. 45).

"The fatal thing is to reduce faith to an explanation. It is not an explanation, it is a passion" (p. 47).

"Sacrifice exposes spiritual fantasy as a masquerade of faith" (p. 49).

"Sacrifice is a readiness to interrupt whatever we are doing and build an altar, bind whatever we happen to be carrying with us at the moment, place it on the altar, and see what God wills to do with it" (p. 49).

"A sacrificial life is the means, and the only means, by which a life of faith matures" (p. 50).

"The temptation is to think that God is there to serve us. The temptation is to come to God as a consumer shopping for the gospel as a commodity. The temptation is to reduce God to a cozy domesticity" (p. 53).

"Our faith, all faith, everyone's faith, needs testing. And we cannot be trusted to test ourselves.... We are too devious in devising ways of cooking the books to document the evidence that serves our illusions" (p. 53).

"The way of faith does not serve our fantasies, our illusions, or our ambitions. Faith is not the way to God on our terms, it is the way of God to us on his terms" (p. 55).

"Untested faith does not yet qualify as faith" (p. 57).

"Faith, repeatedly tested by sacrifice, was a way of life for Abraham. Each sacrifice left him with less of self and more of God. Each sacrifice abandoned something of self on an altar from which he traveled onward with more vision, more promise, more Presence" (p. 58).

Questions for Interaction

1. What is it about Abraham that makes him the "ancestor of all who believe" (Rom. 4:11), the prototype for the way of faith?
2. "Go!" is the first verb of the Abraham story and the culminating command of the Jesus story. Are you going? Where has God told you to go? How is the journey?
3. How do Abraham-like stories of faith provide travel companions that help us live faithfully?
4. The Abraham story is sparsely detailed. How can too much information about how someone lives their life of faith hurt us? How can we handle the temptation to copy instead of improvising ourselves?
5. How is a sacrificial life a slow life in a fast world? In what ways is that good?
6. In what areas of your life have you learned sacrifice? Are there areas in which you're holding back?
7. When you consider your life and your prayers, do you think that you're using God, or are you letting God use you? How might your prayers be different?
8. Testing is essential to weed out our illusions and self-deceptions. What has testing weeded out of you?
9. The life of faith requires testing. Have you ever tried to turn it around and test God? What do you think the consequences have been?

10. What kind of God would God have to be if he catered to our whims, if he obeyed us instead of calling us to obey him?
11. In whom have you seen testing and sacrifice reveal a deeper, more mature faith?
12. It's nice to abandon a checkered past. But are you willing to abandon a promising future for God's sake?

Praying with traveling companions on the Jesus way: Christina Rossetti (1830-1894)

Speak, Lord, for Thy servant heareth. Grant us ears to hear, eyes to see, wills to obey, hearts to love; then declare what Thou wilt, reveal what Thou wilt, command what Thou wilt, demand what Thou wilt.

SESSION 4

Moses: On the Plains of Moab; or, The Named, Storied, Signposted Way of Congregational Scripture Reading

(pp. 59-77)

Summary

Moses, who claimed to be no good with words, has both the most words and the most foundational words in all Scripture ascribed to him. The shepherd who couldn't talk became the preacher who couldn't stop talking.

But scholarship has done the disservice of distancing Moses from the actual writing of the Torah. Three hundred years of scholarship have shown us that it's possible to learn how to pull the Bible apart and never learn how to "drive" it. It is imperative, therefore, to regain the wholeness and oral nature of the scriptures. Though not all the words in the five books of Moses were penned by Moses himself, he is the authority behind and the direction in which they move.

Language theory is helpful here, because it distinguishes between two types of reading. Diachronic ("through time") reading is reading in which we're in control, in which getting information is the goal. Synchronic ("with time") reading is reading in which we submit to the authority of what's written, in which being led by what is revealed is the goal. The "unity and divinity" of the scriptures must be maintained, as every word (even "begat" repeated again and again) is kept together with every other word.

Our speaking is derived from God's speaking. Therefore, words are holy. They create. Peterson says, "Words are inherently holy regardless of their employment, whether we are making up a shopping list, making conversation with an acquaintance on a street corner, praying in the name of Jesus, asking for directions to the bus station, reading the prophet Isaiah, or writing a letter to our congresswoman" (pp. 66-67). This holiness of words requires that we show care and reverence for them. The very health of those who follow the Jesus way rests on how we use words.

The biblical story teaches us how to use words. Peterson reminds us how we should approach this story — not from above, as "presumptuous historical criticism" (p. 68) does, but from below. These words, this Word, has authority over us; we have no authority over it. These words don't enter us, as if we were bigger than them. We enter into them, into their stories, as pilgrims.

According to the biblical story, Moses was both a man of action and a man of words. His actions rescued a people, but his words created a people. His words weren't timeless pronouncements pulled out of the heavens. They were spoken to real people — a real worshiping congregation was created and shaped by them. "The way of language in which Moses is our first teacher," Peterson explains, "[is] the kind of language that develops in a worshiping congregation that invokes God and then listens and prays. It is the language of a community of faith" (p. 69).

"Three elements stand out in the language of revelation used by this community," says Peterson: "names, stories, and signposts" (p 70). Names are the greatest forms of human speech, and they abound in Scripture. All these tongue-tripping names root Scripture in the personal, in real lives. Ideas are important, but particular people rise to the surface.

Names become stories. "A name is a seed," Peterson writes. "When it germinates it becomes a story" (p. 71). And stories are the primary way God's Word comes to us. Unlike ideas, which we can merely think about, stories invite participation. And yet they don't manipulate us or distract us (unless they are propagandizing stories trying to enlist us into causes or sentimental stories trying to seduce us into escaping from life). What they do is engage our imaginations. They show us a different way of living than our culturally conditioned way of living.

Our problem is our experts, who prefer information over stories. The solution: Going back to our biblical stories, which remind us of the importance of our own life stories and our participation in the life of God.

Along with names and stories, Moses offers what Peterson refers to as signposts: "laws are posted, directions given, instructions provided" (p. 73). Some are succinct and punchy; others are elaborate and detailed.

All deal with the challenge of living and worshiping as community, taking great care with how we live and what we believe.

In an age of using words to inform and control, Moses leads us on the named, storied, signposted way of reading Scripture in community.

Key Adjectives

coherent, whole, foundational, cohesive, personal, integrated, oral, revealed, enduring, stable, living, authoritative, Spirit-directed, submissive, anticipating, personal, organic, holistic, webbed, unified, divine, holy, vulnerable, sacred, meaningful, derivative, essential, inherent, healthy, reverent, relational, urgent, robust, vital, empowering, bold, relentless, untiring, congregational, worshiping, listening, praying, formative, complex, consistent, covenantal, promissory, storied, practical, matter-of-fact, reliable, alert, participatory, artistic, moral, imaginative, honest, respectful, large, broad, succinct, punchy, fundamental, basic, detailed, elaborate, intricate

Quotations to Consider

"Words spoken are both previous to and even inherently superior to words written even in the most literate of cultures" (p. 62).

"Words are holy — all words. But words are also vulnerable to corruption, debased into blasphemies, trivialized into gossip" (p. 66).

"By and large reverence for language is not conspicuous among us, in or out of the Christian community" (p. 67).

"If there is going to be a healthy community, there has to be a healthy language" (p. 67).

"Words don't just sit there, like bumps on a log. They have *agency*" (p. 68).

"In our Holy Scriptures story is the primary verbal means for bringing God's word to us" (p. 71).

"Story doesn't just tell us something and leave it there. It invites our participation. A good storyteller gathers us into the story" (p. 72).

"And so when we lose touch with our lives, our *souls* — our moral, bodily, spiritual, God-personal lives — story is the best verbal way of getting us back in touch again" (p. 73).

"Community is intricate and complex. Living in community as a people of God is inherently messy" (p. 74).

"We have an absolute genius for finding whatever might serve as a loophole in the commandments and creed" (p. 75).

"The way language is used — context and syntax, grammatical mood and poetic rhythm — provides the meaning. *God* out of context, without syntax, can be either blessing or blasphemy" (p. 76).

"Impersonal, story-less talk and writing is a blight on the world of discourse. Moses keeps us story-trained, and our lives story-responsive, congregation-rooted, congregation-relational" (p. 76).

Questions for Interaction

1. Have you ever been in a Bible-study group that was more about getting information from the text than living the text? What went wrong? How did that happen?
2. Do you skip the tongue-twisting names when reading Scripture? When was the last time someone skipped or mangled your name? Why are names so important?
3. What does Peterson mean when he says that the biblical stories invite our participation?
4. How have the highly caffeinated stories of TV shows sidelined the biblical stories? What are some nonbiblical stories (told in books, movies, songs, etc.) that have reinvigorated the biblical stories for you?
5. What biblical story captured your imagination recently? How did it show a different, countercultural way of living?
6. Signposts give commands, and they establish conditions for life. What is the difference between the two? How can we tell?

7. What command in Scripture have you recently heard? What has obedience to that command looked like?

8. Peterson refers to the necessity to "ride fence" to keep cattle from getting on the wrong side of the fence. Who do you "ride fence" for? Who "rides fence" for you?

Praying with traveling companions on the Jesus way: Origen (ca. 185-254)

Lord God, let us keep your Scriptures in mind and meditate on them day and night, persevering in prayer, always on the watch. We beg you, Lord, to give us real knowledge of what we read and to show us not only how to understand it, but how to put it into practice, so that we may deserve to obtain spiritual grace, enlightened by the law of the Holy Spirit, through Jesus Christ our Lord, whose power and glory will endure throughout all ages. Amen.

David: "I Did Not Hide My Iniquity";
or, The Imperfect Way of Penitential Prayer

(pp. 78-100)

Religious readers

Summary

Perfectionism is a constant danger, taking us far from the way of Jesus. Theologically, the church throughout history has consistently rejected perfectionism as dividing the body of Christ. And yet it continually rears its ugly head. No generation is without its elitist perfectionists.

Perfectionism seems to be a natural extension of a serious effort to follow Jesus. Anything less that complete devotion seems like a waste of time. And so we impose it on ourselves and everyone else.

But the way of David is the way of imperfection. He brings together the highs and lows of following God in a way that captures the imagination. We see his life from two vantage points: outwardly, in the stories of 1 Samuel 16 through 1 Kings 2; and inwardly, in the prayers of the Psalms. Outside and inside, stories and prayers — both are necessary to understand a person.

The biblical story doesn't sanitize David, doesn't make him a flawless hero. Rather, with all of his flaws and failures, he is presented as representative of what this life of faith is like. David, not perfection, is our guide on the way of prayer.

Peterson's favorite story about David takes place at En-gedi, with its harsh and inhospitable wilderness. It was there that David fled from King Saul, and it was there that David didn't kill the king when he had the chance. Interestingly, David, who had made a career of killing, refused to kill the one man who was hell-bent on killing him. "The reason David's refusal to kill King Saul catches and holds my attention," Peterson explains, "is that it strikes me as completely uncharacteristic of David" (p. 84).

David of the adulterous affair. David the failed father. David the calloused and calculating one. These flaws are matched by admirable traits: David's capacity for deep friendship, his passionate worship of God, and his humble kindness. Peterson comments, "The life of David is a labyrinth of ambiguities, not unlike our own. What we admire in David does not cancel out what we abhor, and what we abhor does not cancel out what we admire" (p. 87).

David is not an example to be copied. "The story of David is not a story of what God wants us to be but a story of God working with the raw material of our lives as he finds us" (p. 88).

We know David through the Psalms as well as his story. Not all of the psalms come from David, but there's an awareness of David throughout the Psalter. Peterson notes, "The Psalms express everything we are capable of experiencing" (p. 89). Most of them are prayed in the context of trouble, and at the center of these are seven penitential prayers offered out of shame and sorrow for sin. Penitential prayers are the antidote for perfectionism.

Psalm 6 connects us with the devastation caused by evil in the world. And then it locates that evil within us, not just "out there." We are part of it.

Psalm 32 connects sin with forgiveness. When caught in sin, we often promise to do better. But promises don't banish sin; God's forgiveness does.

Psalm 38 shows the connection of body and soul by showing how both are affected by sin. "The whole person is involved. There is no inner and outer in matters of sin" (p. 92).

Psalm 51 connects sin with dirt. "Sin, in a sense, has no substance in itself. It can exist only as a perversion or distortion of the good, the true, the beautiful, which it is its genius to defile" (p. 94). It makes us dirty — over and over and over again — making frequent washing, frequent forgiveness, a necessity.

Psalm 102 shows the relational disruption of sin. Sin brings isolation, loneliness, abandonment. Yet, in the midst of disconnection, God is active and present with us, restoring relationship.

Psalm 130 shows how we are incapacitated by sin and find ourselves waiting on the way. Amazingly, our sin "does not disqualify us from be-ing on the way" (pp. 96-97). And the waiting shows that most of what happens on the way isn't done and said by us, but by God.

Psalm 143 moves us from a focus on sin to a focus on God. Being preoccupied with sin is just as bad as ignoring it. Our focus should be on God, not on all those other sinners out there. "It is God's business to take care of the sin" (p. 99).

These seven prayers teach us how to deal with sin. But we can't deal with it ourselves; sin can't be "managed." It can only be forgiven, God-forgiven. We deal with God; God deals with sin.

Prayer restores our God-orientation, moving us away from our self-improvement spiritualities. The way of David is the imperfect way of penitential prayer, not of elite perfectionism.

Key Adjectives

quotidian, daily, inside, outside, normal, genuine, contrite, re-sponsible, forgiven, dirty, relational, quieted, incapacitated, imperfect, penitential

Quotations to Consider

"Perfectionism is a disorder that occurs frequently in the Christian com-munity" (p. 78).

"Perfectionism is a perversion of the Christian way" (p. 79).

"David is a man of God, but not by any means a perfect man of God" (p. 88).

"There are times when an accumulated sense of the sheer mass of trouble in the world just knocks the wind out of us, knocks the *prayer* out of us. . . . Those moments are compounded when we realize that some of the wrong is in us — we are not just observers of it, we are part of it" (pp. 89-90).

"There is much laughter and singing and dancing on this way [of imper-fection], palm branches and hosannas. But there are also tears and la-ments, rivers of them, every tear a prayer and not one unnoticed" (p. 91).

"The great, great grandaddy of all sins is the denial of sin, the refusal to admit sin" (p. 91).

"The only effective remedy for sin is the forgiveness of sin — and only God can forgive sin" (p. 91).

"Confession is a way out of the puny, self-deceiving, mulish contrivances we attempt in order to manage sin on our own. Confession is entrance into the vast world of forgiveness, encompassed with God's deliverance and steadfast love" (p. 92).

"Sin introduces a foreign substance into our souls" (p. 92).

"There is no us and them in matters of sin" (p. 93).

"We can no more live a sinless life than we can plant potatoes without getting our hands dirty" (p. 94).

"We are made for one another. We are not ourselves by ourselves" (p. 95).

"Sin is not a superficial blemish on either soul or body, it penetrates to the depths" (p. 96).

"Sin does not expel us from our place on the way. We may be stuck, incapacitated, lost, depressed, angry, puzzled, confused, but we are still on the way" (p. 97).

"Waiting for the Lord is a large part of what we do on the way because the largest part of what takes place on the way is what God is doing, what God is saying" (p. 97).

"The Holy Spirit is not out recruiting an elite, all-star holiness team for the Jesus way" (p. 100).

Questions for Interaction

1. Have you ever looked down on other Christians who are going about the Christian life in "the wrong way" (wrong denomination, wrong theology, wrong practices . . .)?
2. Do you feel the lure of perfectionism in your own life? How do you deal with it?
3. How can we be passionate without being perfectionistic?

4. How has your faith been derailed or damaged by your own and/or others' pressures to be perfect?
5. How is perfectionism evident outside the church? In what ways do we import it into the church?
6. How do you cope with all the evil and suffering that's evident in the world?
7. Which do you rely on more — willpower or God's forgiveness? Why is willpower so attractive?
8. Why is confession so much less attractive to us than do-it-yourself spirituality?
9. When have you felt the effects of sin in your body (not just your soul)?
10. Are you in waiting mode right now? What are you waiting for?
11. Waiting for the Lord is a large part of the Jesus way. What is it that you need from God in order to get back on the way? Healing? Direction? Forgiveness?
12. Why do we get caught up in the "sin-gossip" and scandals of others while ignoring our own sins?

Praying with traveling companions on the Jesus way: St. Ambrose of Milan (339-397)

O Lord, you who are all merciful, take away my sins from me, and enkindle within me the fire of your Holy Spirit. Take away this heart of stone from me, and give me a heart of flesh and blood, a heart to love and adore you, a heart which may delight in you, love you, and please you, for Christ's sake. Amen.

SESSION 6

Elijah: "Hide Yourself by the Brook Cherith"; or, The Idol-Exposing Way of Prophetic Worship

(pp. 101-26)

Summary

Elijah is the representative prophet in Scripture. He is the one associated with the "preached and proclaimed — prophetic! — word of God that gets our attention and gets us back on the way when we have willfully left it or mindlessly strayed from it" (p. 102).

Prophets call us out of our "god-fantasies and god-lies" (p. 102) and back to worshiping Yahweh. Peterson writes, "Prophets insist that God is the living center or nothing. Our task is to become relevant to his situation. They insist that we deal with God as God reveals himself, not as we imagine him to be" (p. 103).

Prophets do two things. They both "expose the idolatries and compromises of the country and give witness to the word and presence of God" (p. 103). Our idolatry. God's reality.

Just as Elijah's "weather forecast" exposed the impotence of Baal and the barrenness of Asherah, prophetic preaching exposes the impotence and barrennesss of our cultural idolatries. Our religious idolatries offer "religion with all the 'benefits' of instant gratification" (p. 106), not God on his own terms.

While contradicting whatever idolatries are contemporary, prophets develop their biblical identities on the margins. Elijah doesn't prepare for the showdown with the false prophets of Baal by learning as much as he can about Baal and Baalism. He does it by following God's leading into the wilderness and beyond, where he experiences God's provision through the ravens and the widow. "His out-of-the-way life," Peterson suggests, "is foundational to whatever effectiveness he will have when he has the attention of the world.... He is the same man in obscurity as he is in the spotlight" (p. 108).

The heart of Baalism is an indulgence in the senses — it is worship that is controlled by feelings. The adjectives that describe Baal worship are "interesting," "relevant," "exciting." But Elijah and the biblical prophets have one word to describe this kind of worship, "worship that seeks fulfillment through self-expression, worship that accepts the needs and desires and passions of the worshiper as its baseline" (p. 110). That word is "harlotry."

Authentic worship is not being present to our feelings; authentic worship is being present to the living God with all of who we are. This means our senses are included, of course. "But as rich and varied as the sensory life is," Peterson points out, "it is always defined and ordered by the word of God" (p. 111).

Worship is "a response to God's word in the context of the community of God's people" (p. 111). Simply put, this is what divides authentic worship from feelings that are often confused with worship. It is something we do, not something we experience.

Elijah retraces Moses' steps. The formation of the people of God by the Word (given by Moses) isn't enough. The reformation of the people of God by the Word needs to be done through the prophetic voice (such as Elijah's) over and over and over again. That reformational call will always be to obey and serve the God we have been trying to get to obey and serve us.

As Elijah shows, the prophet refuses to divide the world between the sacred and the secular. He or she speaks the Name into every corner of life. Everything is sacred. There is nowhere that is God-free.

There are also no God-free relationships. "For the prophet, God is as real as the next-door neighbor; the neighbor is as real as God" (p. 120). Loving God and loving one's neighbor are completely inseparable.

We like to talk about "making room for God," Peterson says. But God doesn't fit into our lives. He's much too big. "If we want anything to do with God," Peterson writes, "we have to fit into him and the men and women he places alongside us" (p. 122).

The prophet's task will never be easy. Baal worship is intoxicating and addictive. If you've got a god at your beck and call, why give him up?

28

But the prophet will continue to beat the drum of God, revelation, and community, leading us in worship that heads in a direction exactly the opposite of whatever culture we find ourselves in.

The Jesus way is the idol-exposing way of prophetic worship.

Key Adjectives

recovering, preaching, proclaiming, prophetic, powerful, skilled, fiery, passionate, immersed, energetic, imaginative, undiluted, cowardly, attentive, prayerful, abrupt, brief, particular, personal, surprised, unlikely, marginal, secluded, isolated, silent, unpopular, undiplomatic, tactless, unceremonious

Quotations to Consider

"[Elijah] was immersed in the culture and politics of his day but not shaped by them. . . . His energy and imagination were undiluted by opinion polls and proffered compromises" (p. 104).

"[Elijah] knows how to obey orders, even when the orders make no sense (maybe especially when the orders make no sense). He goes where God directs him and finds himself cared for" (p. 108).

"A divine will that sets itself in opposition to the sin-tastes and self-preoccupations of humanity is incomprehensible in Baalism and so is impatiently discarded" (p. 110).

"Authentic worship means being present to the living God who penetrates the whole of human life" (p. 110).

"Biblically formed people of God do not use the term 'worship' as a description of experience, such as 'I can have a worship experience with God on the golf course.' What that means is, 'I can have religious feelings reminding me of good things, awesome things, beautiful things nearly any place.' Which is true enough. The only thing wrong with the statement is its ignorance, thinking that such experience makes up what the Christian church calls worship" (p. 111).

"Worship in the biblical sources and in liturgical history is not something a person *experiences,* it is something we *do,* regardless of how we feel about it, or whether we feel anything about it at all. The experience develops out of the worship, not the other way around" (p. 111).

"In Yahwism worship is defined and shaped by God's authoritative and clear word. Nothing is dependent on feelings or weather. All is determined by Scripture and Jesus. No person is left to do what he or she simply feels like doing. God has revealed who he is and demands obedience. Worship is the act of attending to that revelation and being obedient to it" (p. 112).

"If we have a choice, which we do, of dealing with God or an image of God, we much prefer the image" (p. 116).

"There are innumerable ways in which we can make a god-image that suits our individual style of spirituality. The possibilities are endless. . . . It is no wonder that idol-making and idol-worshiping continue to be the most popular religious game in town" (p. 117).

"The task of the prophet is to say the name God correctly, accurately and locally — *Yahweh,* God alive, God personal, God present" (p. 119).

"One of the bad habits that we pick up early in our lives is separating things and people into secular and sacred. . . . Prophets will have none of this. They hold that everything, absolutely everything, takes place on sacred ground" (p. 120).

"Prophets make it difficult for us to evade God or make detours around God after we leave church or temple or synagogue. Prophets insist on receiving God and dealing with God in every nook and cranny of life" (p. 120).

"Because he lived on the margins [Elijah] was unimpressed by what went on in the center" (p. 121).

"There is an addictive quality to Baal. Giving up Baal means that we give up control over God" (p. 125).

Questions for Interaction

1. Under Ahab's father Omri, the standard of living increased, but spirituality went to pot. In what ways is this also an apt description of North American reality?
2. Baalism was a full-on sensory experience. What protects worship in your church from slipping into an indulgence in the senses?
3. What is your worship like? If you think it is more feelings-based than God-based, what might you do to change that?
4. In what ways are the images, ideas, and characteristics of God that are dear and powerful to us ultimately distortions of who God really is?
5. When we thoughtlessly reduce God from a person to an idea, what happens to our praying? To our worship? To living a holy life?
6. In what ways does your church worship counteract the Baal idolatries of our time? Are there ways in which it capitulates to them?
7. Worship always connects us with revelation. Elijah retraced the steps of Moses. Does our worship retrace the steps of Moses? Of Jesus? What would retracing these steps look like?
8. Are there ways in which you have ensconced God in sacred places and events, leaving yourself in (apparent) control of everything else? What are you willing to do to change this situation?
9. How does worshiping a personal God help keep all of our relationships personal (as opposed to functional)?
10. Peterson writes, "For the prophet, God is as real as the next-door neighbor; the neighbor is as real as God" (p. 120). How does this square with your experience?

Praying with traveling companions on the Jesus way: Albrecht Dürer (1471-1528)

O God in heaven, have mercy on us! Lord Jesus Christ, intercede for your people, deliver us at the opportune time, preserve in us the true, genuine Christian faith, collect your scattered sheep with your voice, your divine Word, as Holy Writ calls it. Help us to recognize your voice, help us not to be allured by the madness of the world, so that we may never fall away from you, O Lord Jesus Christ. Amen.

SESSION 7

Isaiah of Jerusalem: "The Holy";
or, The Obedient Way of Holy Living

(pp. 127-48)

Note

Biblical scholars tend to divide the book of Isaiah into two or three main sections that they believe were written during different time periods and by different authors, though the second (and possibly third) author(s) preached and wrote in intentional continuity with the first author. Accordingly, the book of Isaiah is held together by an essential unity. Peterson subscribes to the three-author theory. In this chapter he focuses on the first author, referred to as Isaiah of Jerusalem. In the next chapter he focuses on the second author, referred to as the Prophet of the Exile.

Summary

Most of us have a limited — and limiting — understanding of the word "holy." But in company with Isaiah of Jerusalem, we discover something completely different. As we travel the way with him, we discover that "'holy' is the best word we have for the all-encompassing, all-embracing life of God that transforms us into a uniquely formed and set-apart people" (p. 127).

Boring, banal, safe — that's what many make of holiness: "goodness in a straitjacket, truth drained of mystery, beauty emasculated into ceramic knickknacks" (p. 128). But, Peterson reminds us, "holiness is in wild and furious opposition to all such banality and blandness" (p. 128). The Holy is both magnificent and dangerous. Glorious and deadly.

Preceding the "Holy, holy, holy" of the angels in Isaiah 6 is the mention of the death of King Uzziah. Uzziah was a great king, except . . . As Peterson puts it, "He decided to take charge of his own spirituality, manage his own religion, put God to his own uses" (p. 130). But trying to manage The Holy, to control God, is folly at best. Peterson likens dealing with The Holy to walking through grizzly country: "Holy ground, but dangerous ground" (p. 131).

So, how do we approach The Holy if it's so wonderful and yet so uncontrollably dangerous? By being present to the Presence. By following Isaiah's example and going to church not for our own purposes, but to pray and worship.

To fully enter into The Holy requires a biblical imagination, a sense of the scope of what God has done in the past and intends to do in the future. Otherwise, "we run the risk of confining The Holy to what takes place in the sanctuary at a scheduled time" (p. 133).

Moses in the bleak desert and John on austere Patmos and Isaiah in the desecrated temple — The Holy is at home in the most unsuspecting places. It's essential that we get this into our imaginations, because so often we look at the conditions around us, throw up our hands, and say, "Holiness certainly can't happen here." We do this in our countries, our denominations, our churches, our homes, and our own lives. But God's holiness cannot be controlled or excluded or contained. The Holy cannot be reduced to special times, special places, or special people.

Contrary to what we read in the newspapers or online, that's not what's really going on. The Holy is going on. God is going on.

The Holy is not something to watch. It is something to participate in. Uusally that participation begins with "an overwhelming sense of inadequacy" (p. 135). When Isaiah sees The Holy, he becomes aware of his unclean lips. The first thing we are aware of when we enter into The Holy is our own lack of holiness. We are sinful, unworthy. "The excess of life makes me aware of my deficit of life" (p. 136).

Our awareness of sin opens up the ability to receive mercy, to be purified, as Isaiah was purified. The chapter on David showed us that sin is not *something* that we can control, and the chapter on Elijah showed us that God is not *someone* that we can control. This chapter on Isaiah shows us what happens when the sin we can't control is met by the God we can't control: purification. Holiness moves from something outside of us to something inside of us.

Holiness doesn't end with personal purification. It calls us "to enter into what God is doing and intending to get done in the world. And it's for everyone" (p. 137). There is no coercion involved here: we are invited to participate in God's holiness work.

Drawing on Isaiah's story, Peterson notes four elements involved in participating in The Holy: "the abolition of self-sufficiency . . . , the experience of merciful forgiveness . . . , God's invitation to servant work . . . , and the human response of becoming present to God in faith and obedience" (p. 137).

It is important to note that, while these elements are in no particular order or proportion, there are "no exceptions in Scripture or church in which these elements are not present, whether explicitly or implicitly" (p. 137). And as much as we'd like to turn them into a program, they defy technique because they can't be removed from their context. What we do know is that worshiping God helps us acquire "readiness and perceptiveness for the holy" (p. 137).

Having heard the call to participate in The Holy, we hear the second half of the call: the stump. The conclusion of Isaiah's vision shows a stump in a field of stumps. He is called to bring God's message to people who are deaf and blind as stumps. And Isaiah, the greatest preacher in Scripture, is also the greatest failure. Nobody listens.

Like Isaiah, we are called to proclaim the good news of God to stump-like people. But the stump in the field of stumps, Peterson reminds us, is "the holy seed" (Isa. 6:13) — Jesus. "The same Holy, Holy, Holy that filled the temple is a holy seed in the field of stumps" (p. 146). The "holy stump" brings beauty out of ugliness, life out of death.

Key Adjectives

Holy, comprehensive, lived, all-encompassing, all-embracing, invigorating, precious, wild, furious, extravagant, spontaneous, fiery, passionate, exuberant, deep, good, true, beautiful, magnificent, life-giving, life-enhancing, life-deepening, energetic, dangerous, risky, authentic, undiluted, firsthand, attractive, intense, large, expansive, surprising, transformative, obscure, dazzling, dramatic, ignored, glorious, absent, healed, restored, ransomed, forgiven, unlikely, unmanageable, irrepressible, hidden, abundant, inconvenient, baffling, disappointing, non-negotiable

Quotations to Consider

"Holy is never a pious abstraction. . . . It is the life of God breathed into and invigorating our lives" (p. 127).

"The holy is an interior fire, a passion for living in and for God, a capacity for exuberance in the presence of God" (p. 128).

"The authoritative source for understanding the holy so that we can participate in the holy is Holy Scripture inspired by Holy Spirit" (pp. 128-29).

"Hanging around the holy is risky business. Holy ground is dangerous ground" (p. 131).

"The Holy is never, never something of God that we can take as if we owned it and use for our own purposes" (p. 131).

"Holy, Holy, Holy is not Christian needlepoint" (p. 132).

"We need all of Scripture, all of history, all of experience to provide a horizon large enough to take in The Holy. The Holy cannot be cramped into a shoe box. The Holy cannot be perceived through a peephole" (p. 134).

"The unique thing about the holy is that it cannot be known or understood apart from entering it, apart from being formed by The Holy. It is not a subject we learn from a book or a lecture. We enter in. . . . And there are no shortcuts" (p. 135).

"Holiness cannot be reduced to an emotional, devotional experience that we cultivate in order to 'feel spiritual'" (p. 137).

"God's call is spoken as a question, inviting response; we have the freedom of a yes or a no. However impelling this word is to some of us, it is never a matter of coercion. We are *invited* in" (p. 137).

"Wherever we are, whatever we are doing, there is *more*, and the more is God, revealing himself in Jesus by the Spirit, the *Holy* Spirit" (p. 138).

"Holiness is transformative, although rarely sudden" (p. 138).

"God cannot be accounted for by what we imagine God might be. God cannot be argued into belief by philosophical reasoning. God cannot be explained or interpreted by notions we have acquired by assembling feelings of reverence from sunsets, spiked with a few stories of miracles, and then legitimated with some comments that we pick up from celebrity interviews" (p. 141).

"Because of who God is, *The Holy*, we have to let God tell us who he is. If we insist on using *our* ideas to form our image of God, we will get it all wrong" (p. 141).

"The fact is that men and women have no love or taste for The Holy — they want a God who serves them on their terms, not a God they can serve on his terms" (p. 143).

"All of us, if we only knew it, are on a hunt for the holy, for a life that cannot be reduced to the way we look or what we do or what others think of us" (p. 147).

Questions for Interaction

1. Do you have a sense of glorious wonder when you enter worship? How about a sense of life-risking danger? In what ways might you need to broaden and enrich your sense of The Holy?
2. How do the things we buy in Christian bookstores/gift shops help us attend to The Holy? How might some of these things trivialize The Holy?
3. Does the word "holiness" have a personal feel to you? Explain.
4. In what ways can holiness be an invitation to do God's work?
5. Peterson discusses the four elements of holiness: the abolition of self-sufficiency, the experience of merciful forgiveness, God's invitation to servant work, and the human response of becoming present to God in faith and obedience. What is your experience of each of these elements?
6. Think of the way your church goes about being church. In what ways is it market-driven?
7. If churches keep insisting on being god-marketers, is it any wonder that our culture continues to be one of god-consumers? Are there

features in your church's approach to membership that contribute to god-consumption?

8. Do you ever get the sense that what God has called you to is like speaking to old stumps? How does Isaiah's call help you make sense of your own?

9. Share what Peterson would call a "Stump Town story." Where have you seen God take something old and dead and bring something new and holy to life?

Praying with traveling companions on the Jesus way: St. Anselm (1033-1109)

O Lord our God, grant us grace to desire you with a whole heart, that so desiring you we may seek and find you, and so finding you may love you, and loving you may hate those sins which separate us from you, for the sake of Jesus Christ. Amen.

SESSION 8

Isaiah of the Exile: "How Beautiful on the Mountains"; or, The Beautiful Way of Servant Evangelism

(pp. 149-89)

Summary

The destruction of Jerusalem and the Exile in Babylon meant the end of the kingdom, the end of the temple worship. The people of God were humiliated. All evidence seemed to point to a horrifying conclusion: God had abandoned them — in fact, God was dead. Marduk had defeated Yahweh.

A painful time of emptiness is a necessary part of transformation. Taking off dirty, tattered clothes in order to put on splendid garments still leaves you naked in between. Sometimes, silence is necessary in order to hear again. That was the Exile: a time to be stripped of all vestiges of illusion and pretension, a time to listen.

Then, finally, a voice. Picking up where the ignored Isaiah of Jerusalem left off, 150 years later the Prophet of the Exile cultivated the seeds that had been sowed. The Prophet spoke, and what he said was good news — gospel. But gospel isn't just the announcement of good news. "It brings us into a participating awareness of what it proclaims — God himself active and present in his word and we ourselves *involved*, whether we want to be or not" (p. 161). Gospel proclamation is about God, not us.

The Prophet's proclamation has three elements: "images of God for the people of God" (p. 163), ridicule of false gods, and biblical foundations for his proclamations, foundations from the Genesis creation and the Exodus salvation.

The images of God don't prove God's existence. They show his personal presence. Mostly what they show is God creating and God saving. "Creation is the theater; covenant is the salvation that is played out in the theater" (pp. 164-65). People need new images to see God alive and at work, creating and saving.

While enlarging our imagination of God, the Prophet shows our "no-god" idolatries for what they are. "His ridicule is withering, merciless" (p. 166), but it serves a good purpose: the clearing of clouded imaginations.

But to keep these newly cleansed and enlarged imaginations from being something purely internal and spiritualized, the Prophet ties them to the great acts of God in creation and salvation. Spiritualizing would ruin everything he is after. As Peterson explains, "Spiritualizing the gospel means that we love God but not the world that 'God so loved'" (p. 168). But when we connect our imaginations with what God has done in the past, we begin to realize that what God has done before he can and will do again.

That salvation is on its way, that God will rescue us is not surprising. But how he does it is surprising: through a servant. Surprise is a common ingredient in God's way of salvation. Surprise always forces us to choose between our ideas about God and how he ought to work and our faith in God himself. And the word "servant" keeps popping up in Scripture and surprising us.

While the Hebrews were freed from Egyptian slavery, they were still slaves. "What changed, the only thing that changed, was that they had a different Master, Yahweh the Lord of life instead of Pharaoh the tyrant of death" (p. 173).

The Prophet gives us four "servant songs" that identify "the servant and/or servants that God will use to save his people from their Babylonian exile" (p. 174). The Servant is Jesus, but Peterson notes that as we follow the way of Jesus, these servant songs describe us every bit as much as they described him.

The work of the servant in the songs is not what we hoped for. Yes, it is ultimately victorious, but it is a way that attracts scorn and looks like failure. The way of the servant is the way of sacrifice.

The suffering of the servant isn't tragic. It's chosen. It's sacrifice. Vicarious suffering. Suffering not for his own sins but for the sins of others. "The servant personally *takes* the wrongdoer and the wrong to the altar of sacrifice and makes an offering of him or her on it" (p. 177).

In his life and on the cross, "Jesus was at one and the same time God and servant" (p. 179). While the way of Jesus was and is unique, we are called to participate in it. "The cross on Golgotha . . . is unrepeatable — but cross *bearing* is not. . . . We can — we *must* — participate in Jesus' work the way Jesus did it and does it and only in the way Jesus did and does it, obedient and joyful servants as we follow our servant Savior" (p. 179).

As true as this is, it's not something we are drawn to. In fact, "the way of the servant has rarely, maybe never, been a well-traveled way in the Christian community" (p. 180). In fact, we prefer the way the world tries to fix itself: through education (*teaching* people to do what's right) and, if that doesn't work, through law enforcement (*making* people do what's right and punishing them if they don't).

But the way of the servant isn't just the way of suffering; it's the beautiful way. Not beauty as an ornament to dress up the ugly truth, but beauty as fundamental, as "evidence of and witness to the inherent wholeness and goodness of who God is and the way God works" (p. 181).

"The distinctive thing about beauty," Peterson says, "is that it *reveals*, reveals the depths of what is just beneath the surface, and connects the remote with the present" (p. 183). The problem is that many look on beauty and just don't see it. Those who refuse to follow the way of Jesus won't see it either in him or in his way, even though it's right there.

The work of the evangelist that we get in on is to proclaim the beautiful news, to make plain what is right there, to show people what's really going on, to invite them to be a part of it.

Again, we cannot do what Jesus did, but "we can enter the way of Jesus' cross and become participants in Jesus' reconciliation of the world. Salvation is not escape from what is wrong but a deep, reconciling embrace of all that is wrong" (p. 184). Instead of condemning sin and sinners, we follow Jesus and go the way of the cross, becoming "fellow-sufferers and participants in the sacrificial life of Jesus" as he takes the sins of the world on himself (p. 184). Light embraces everything that had been shrouded by darkness and claims it as its own. The Old Testament sacrifices weren't just images of what had to happen *for us*, but of what we are to endure *for others*.

Proclaiming the good news is not something we can do in an any-means-possible pragmatic way. We must do it in the Jesus way, the beautifully sacrificial way. And, as the Prophet frequently reminds us, this means paying attention and using our imagination, seeing not just the suffering of the sacrifice, but the beauty of the salvation in it. It also requires consciously cultivating memory, so that we don't experience what's going on now in isolation from what God has been doing throughout history.

Key Adjectives

Empty, absent, naked, silent, passionate, intense, personal, relational, imaginative, nuanced, colorful, kaleidoscopic, withering, merciless, scathing, alert, competent, trusting, obeying, honoring, unnamed, quiet, gentle, despised, abhorred, scorned, unflinching, chosen, equipped, assigned, sacrificial, suffering, vicarious, embracing, accepting, submitting, humiliated, judged, dead, godforsaken, beautiful, excessive, adorational, attentive, coherence, radiant

Quotations to Consider

"When language is devalued, cheapened by generations of propaganda, silence is the only context in which it can be purified of its pollutants" (p. 154).

"Teaching tells us what we need to know and do; it is about us. Preaching tells us who God is and what he does; it is about God" (p. 162).

"Preaching that is primarily about us is not *gospel* preaching; in fact, it is not preaching at all. That would be bad news, not good news" (p. 163).

"Creator and Savior are the outside and inside of Yahweh. The meaning of Creation is to prepare a place in which the will of God will be done. Creation is the external basis for the covenant; the covenant is the internal basis of creation" (p. 165).

"God works in us, but not in us abstracted from creation and history" (p. 169).

"Servants — menial servants, believe it or not — are God's choice to implement the great act of salvation" (p. 170).

"Prophetic preaching is useless if it is not accompanied by prophetic listening" (p. 170).

"Nobody aspires to be a servant. We have a higher opinion of ourselves" (p. 171).

"The servant serves God by serving the sinner, by taking the sinner's place, taking the consequences of sin, doing for the sinner what he or she is helpless to do for himself, herself" (p. 177).

"Much as we try to get out of it or find a way around it, there is simply no following Jesus that does not involve suffering and rejection and death. No exceptions" (p. 178).

"Sin is redeemed not by scrubbing it out of existence but by taking it in as a sacrifice" (p. 184).

"We have to radically revise our imaginations and memories in order to take this in: to see sacrifice, offering, weakness, and suffering as essential, not an option, to salvation" (p. 184).

"There can be no violence or propaganda on the way of the Lord. Life on the way is never violent. Sin is not rejected, it is *borne,* carried in an act of intercession" (p. 185).

"If we decide to follow Jesus and live as servants, we cannot do it in the world's way. Not merely must not, *cannot*" (p. 185).

"Imagination is required to see all that is involved in what is right before our eyes, to see the surface but also to penetrate beneath the surface. Appearances both conceal and reveal: imagination is our means of discerning one from the other so that we get the whole picture" (p. 186).

Questions for Interaction

1. Spend some time thinking of new images of God from your everyday life that will open your eyes to what he is doing now. How do these images help? What happens if you take them too far?
2. The servant passages are generally considered to refer to Jesus and to him alone. What do you think of the idea that they might refer to

you too? How does this change the way you think about what it means to be a Christian?

3. The servant serves by suffering. What are you currently suffering? How might it be a part of the suffering servant work that God has given you?

4. What do you think of the idea that following Jesus has less to do with making your life better now than with suffering for the salvation of others?

5. The servant suffers for the sake of others' sins, not his own. Think about one of the times when you suffered for doing what was right. How did you handle it?

6. When Jesus says that we are to suffer and take up our crosses as we follow him, we tend to spiritualize his words. How do you respond to the prospect of facing physical suffering and even death as you follow Jesus?

7. The Servant/Jesus doesn't reject either the sinner or the sin; he embraces the sinner and bears the sin. Are there some obvious sins and sinners that you tend to reject? If so, what would it be like to bear and embrace them?

8. Pragmatism assumes that ends justify our unfortunately messy means. Where in your life are you tempted to compromise your means to achieve a good-seeming end?

9. How can suffering be beautiful? Share a story of beautiful suffering.

Praying with traveling companions on the Jesus way: Kim Hiett (1966-)

Lord of all nations, whose greatest desire is to draw children to himself, make me this day a mirror to your world, reflecting your love for your children, that my eyes would be opened to the power of your sacrificial redemption through your Son, Jesus. By this name alone do we confidently bring the desires of our hearts. Amen.

PART II

Other Ways

"Spirituality" is hot stuff these days. Everyone wants it. Everyone has it. In fact, in a DIY age, everyone is making their own kind of spirituality.

As Peterson notes, "The way of Jesus is not the only way to live" (p. 194). There are alternatives. The tough thing is that some (many?) of these alternatives are done in the name of Jesus — but not in the *way* of Jesus. Such faulty followings in particular erode and pervert the way of Jesus.

The second part of this book deals with other ways that the earliest Christians had before them, ways they rejected. Each chapter focuses on a person — Herod, Caiaphas, Josephus — and a movement — Pharisees, Essenes, Zealots — that offered a way counter to the Jesus way. And, as you might expect, these kinds of people and movements are all still very much alive and well and with us today, offering alternatives to the Jesus way that are attracting many followers.

In Part I, Scripture established the ways of following Jesus. In Part II, prayer clears away the alternative ways that can obscure our true path.

SESSION 9

The Way of Herod;
or, Avoiding the Detours of Success and Piety

(pp. 197-219)

Summary

Herod dominated the Jewish scene during the half-century leading up to the birth of Jesus. He was wealthy, powerful, and successful. His kingship, which ended with his death in the year of Jesus' birth, is in marked contrast to Jesus' kingship.

But here is what's so interesting about these two: As different as they were, both Jesus and Herod wanted the same thing: the world. Both were establishing kingdoms. While Herod was setting up an earthly kingdom in which he was king, Jesus was setting up the heavenly kingdom in which he was King.

But even though they had similar goals, Jesus completely ignored Herod and what he had accomplished. Why? Sure, their kingdoms were different, but couldn't Jesus at least learn from and borrow some of Herod's methods, since they seemed to be so successful? No. "Jesus ignored the world of power and accomplishment that was brilliantly on display all around him" (p. 204).

Where everything that Herod did was secular and impersonal, everything that Jesus did was saturated with God and intimately personal.

"Herod was impressive; Herod was effective; Herod was successful. But Herod was also secular and godless" (p. 206). For many Jews, prosperity and peace at the cost of losing God wasn't worth it. And that's where this chapter's countermovement comes in: the Pharisees.

Some back history is important here. Following Socrates, Plato, and

47

Aristotle, Alexander the Great was the fourth philosopher, but he spread Greek philosophy by the sword. He was a missionary for all things Greek: intelligence, beauty, pleasure, humanism, civilization. Just like Americanization, Hellenization was hugely successful in winning the world. It was even quite effective in converting many Jews. But not all.

There was a significant rebellion among the Jews. They were God's people. God had made a covenant with them and given them commands. "As Jews, they had no faith in the human as such. Their faith was in God, a jealous God who fiercely rejected manmade substitutes to his revealed justice and love, his mercy and salvation" (p. 208). To them, Greek humanism was blasphemy.

Gradually, this rebellion coalesced into an opposition party: the Pharisees, meaning "separated ones." "Pharisees were Jews at their passionate and loyal best" (p. 210). But over time, their courage and devotion became rigid. By the time of Herod, Peterson describes them as having become "religious crustaceans: all their bone structure was on the outside" (p. 210). Having had to fight to retain their Jewish practices, their identities became tied to what was external, not internal. They became "small-minded, obsessively concerned with all the minute details of personal behavior" (p. 211).

In Jesus' resistance to Herod and his establishment of God's kingdom, the Pharisees seemed like the logical allies: they had a devotion that Herod lacked. But, as Peterson notes, "Jesus no more took his cue from the intensity of the Pharisees than he did from the grandiosity of Herod" (p. 212).

The first thing we notice about Jesus, as those who met him did, is how relational he was. To maintain that, he avoided the "Herod world" of size and numbers and operated in a more modest, quiet world, a world of personal connections.

Then we notice the way he talked, using stories, which create "involvement and relationship" (p. 213). Unlike the Pharisees, who used words to "define and defend" (p. 214), making rules and regulations — in other words, making the world smaller — Jesus used words to make life larger, deeper, more complex and wonderful. Instead of making rules that were precise and limiting, Jesus told stories that were metaphorical and broadening.

Metaphors, as Peterson points out, are actually lies. "You are the salt of the earth" is not literally true. But metaphors are lies that get at the truth in ways that precision can't. They invite participation by engaging the imagination. They draw us into a "web of meanings" (p. 215) as opposed to a single definition.

The way of Jesus keeps us from the alternate ways of Herod and the Pharisees by keeping us in prayer. "The more object-like, the more thing-like, the more impersonal we become, the more disengaged we are from our God-created humanity and from the God-created people around us, the more we need prayer" (p. 217). When we've started turning others into "its," praying with Jesus returns each one to a "you."

Of all the prayers of those along the Jesus way, Peterson recommends the prayer that Mary offered when the angel told her that she would bear Jesus (Luke 1:38). It echoes Jesus' own prayer in the Garden of Gethsemane (Luke 22:42). It is responsive, believing, obeying. It is not the supplication of an egomaniacal Herod; it is the prayer of a servant. "The more exalted we become, the more prominent the position in which we are placed, and the more important we become in the economy of the kingdom of God, the more subservient we become" (p. 218). It is a prayer of submission, not one of pharisaical arrogance.

Between the impressive success of the Herod way and the passionate precision of the Pharisee way is the modestly personal praying of Mary on the Jesus way.

Key Adjectives

Herod: big, large, intoxicating, tallest, important, wealthy, powerful, in-your-face, elaborate, famous, impressive, lavish, violent, conspicuous, skilled, shrewd, immense, majestic, extravagant, prosperous, influential, grandiose

Pharisees: devout, prominent, courageous, loyal, passionate, uncompromising, radical, believing, separated, obsessive, small-minded, external, proud, vigorous, fierce, sincere, strong, determined, intense, serious, colorless, no-nonsense, defined, literal-minded, precise, exact, impersonal

Jesus: obscure, quiet, out-of-the-way, marginal, unimportant, weak, disturbed, powerless, small, intimate, personal, singular, original, radical, intricate, modest

Quotations to Consider

"What I want to insist upon in this is that Jesus did not work out his way of life in the intensely personal and God-oriented small towns . . . simply because he didn't know any better, because that was the only world he knew. No, he *chose* them" (p. 206).

"Imagine yourself moving into a house with a huge picture window. . . . Keeping the window clean develops into an obsessive-compulsive neurosis. You accumulate ladders and buckets and squeegees. You construct a scaffolding both inside and out to make it possible to get at all the difficult corners and heights. You have the cleanest window in North America — but it's now been years since you looked through it. You've become a Pharisee" (p. 211).

"[Phariseeism is the] slow change from an interior passion to an exterior performance and the shift of attention from the majesty of God to housecleaning for God" (p. 212).

"A story is the use of words that creates involvement and relationship. Stories take the stuff of our everyday lived life and carry us into the actions that constitute our experience" (p. 213).

"Storytellers imagine alternate ways of living, wake up our imaginations to who we are and who our neighbors are in fresh ways. We are stimulated to live more intensely, with more awareness" (p. 214).

"Following Jesus necessarily means getting his ways and means into our everyday lives. . . . Jesus' ways are meant to be embraced by our imaginations and assimilated into our habits. This takes place only as we *pray* our following of him. It cannot be imposed from without, cannot be copied. It must be shaped from within. This shaping takes place in prayer" (pp. 216-17).

"Left to ourselves we are a fragmented and distracted people, jerky and spasmodic. Sin does that to us" (p. 217).

"Mary prays God's action into her life. . . . The action is not anything that Mary will do on her own. It is what God will do in Mary. It is that to which she submits. She embraces the action of God" (p. 219).

Questions for Interaction

1. In what ways do Christians today fall into the "Herod trap" of going after what's big and successful? Are there ways in which you fall into it?

2. When have you been influenced by those who have done things effectively, only to discover that the cost of being effective in that way was far too high?

3. Who most impresses you right now? Who impressed you ten years ago? Are you still impressed by them?

4. How do you measure success in your personal life? In ministry?

5. Are you more drawn to success or to passion? In other words, are you more likely to be a Herodian or a Pharisee? How might you moderate — or possibly even change — this tendency?

6. Peterson tells the story of a person who becomes so obsessed with keeping a window clean that he forgets that the window's primary purpose is to show him the majestic view outside. Are there certain external observances of faith whose real purposes have been obscured by your zeal to keep them?

7. Is the way you talk about God more precise and defined, or is it more storied and metaphorical? What do you think is the most fruitful way to talk about God?

8. Why is the Bible so filled with metaphors? Why do metaphors communicate so well what God has to say to us?

9. More than anything else, the way we pray reveals who we are and the way we live. There are three kinds of prayer discussed in this chapter: assertive and demanding prayer (following the way of Herod), "separating" prayer (following the way of the Pharisees), and submissive and willingly obedient prayer (following the way of Mary). How can we ask God for what we need individually and communally and still follow the example set by Mary?

Praying with traveling companions on the Jesus way: St. Teresa of Ávila (1515-1582)

From silly devotions and from sour-faced saints, good Lord, deliver us. Amen.

SESSION 10

The Way of Caiaphas;
or, Avoiding the Detours of Comfort and Elitism

(pp. 220-42)

Summary

Caiaphas is a bookend to Herod. Where Herod the politician enters the Jesus story at the birth, Caiaphas the priest enters it at the death. And despite their many differences, both men agreed upon one thing: Jesus was a threat who needed to be killed.

We don't know nearly as much about Caiaphas as we do about Herod. But this much we do know: "Caiaphas was the most prominent and powerful religious leader in Palestine during the years that Jesus was making his way around the country telling people, 'Follow me'" (p. 221).

Priests are important to our lives, Peterson says. "We are created by God for God. We carry the stamp of God in the very fibers of our body and soul" (p. 222). Because of this God-orientation built into us, we deal with God. And priests help us deal with God because we need help. Left to our own devices, we prefer to be our own gods; we like to keep God in the background. Priests reconnect us with God, presenting God to us and us to the real God.

The giving-and-receiving connection that priests make between God and us is what we call worship. And the heart of worship is sacrifice. There is no worship without sacrifice. The size of the sacrifice is unimportant; it's the quality that matters. The sacrifice doesn't have to be much, "but it does have to be the best we can offer" (p. 223).

Scripture is absolutely full of meticulous details and attention given to worship, from Genesis to Revelation. This is central to who we are and what we do. And Caiaphas was right in the middle of it, bungling things up. And he was in a long line of bunglers. Some priests before him were idolaters, some sensualists, some obstructors of God's Word. But there were also good examples among the bad. What divides them is this rule of thumb: "Priests are at their best when we don't notice them. . . . Their anonymity suggests their authenticity" (p. 226).

Caiaphas was far from anonymous. The line of priests he came from was politicized and secularized, and he outdid all who had come before him, living high on the hog (pun intended).

Obviously, the way of Caiaphas was far from the way of Jesus. But in distinguishing himself from Caiaphas, Jesus didn't work outside the religious system of his day. He wasn't impressed by the temple, but he didn't boycott it, either. Synagogue worship was routine for him.

We should take our cue from Jesus. With all the Caiaphas-like corruption that keeps finding its way into institutional Christianity these days, it's easy for us to want to abandon the whole thing and go it alone, with perhaps a few like-minded friends for company. But, as noxious as it can be, institutional Christianity is necessary and unavoidable if we are to be more than "self-indulgent and subjective and one-generational" (p. 232). The institution is like the dead bark that protects the life of a tree.

The Essenes chose not to follow Jesus' example. The way of the Essenes was a rejection of corrupt religious institutions in favor of a radical purity in what amounted to an alternate world. The Essenes gave up on the bad city (Jerusalem) and its bad religion (the temple) and set out to do things the right way all by themselves. They were "simple, focused, morally pure, scripturally exact" (p. 235) — spiritual elites. "They were the green berets of the kingdom, the special forces. They were a highly trained, highly disciplined, single-minded community of men who had no sympathy with sloth or sloppiness or sin" (p. 236).

Along with rejecting spoiled religion, they rejected a spoiled world and sought to escape both. Retreating to the desert, they were getting ready to escape history as well. Focused on the end times, they controlled their behavior and predicted God's. "They were a sect in the classic sense: no mystery and no ambiguity. They were in control" (p. 237).

Where the sloppiness and self-indulgence of the way of Caiaphas rules the religious institution, the decisive actions and moral clarity of the way of the Essenes will always draw followers.

But we must remember the alternate way of Jesus. While he despised the corruption in the temple, he didn't neglect worshiping there. And while his teaching is marked by a high moral call, he mingled freely with notorious sinners. Instead of gathering a band of spiritual elites, he ended up with a ragtag bunch of losers. But that was his goal. "Jesus wasn't after the best but the worst. He came to seek and to save the lost" (p. 239).

Following Jesus' example, we need to avoid the extremes of the way of Caiaphas and the way of the Essenes. Rather than the non-spirituality of Caiaphas, we need open, trusting worship. Rather than the know-it-all spirituality of the Essenes, we need a not-knowing-everything obedience. Our exemplar here, our praying companion on the Jesus way, is Thomas. Thomas captures worship and obedience in their simplest, truest forms in his five-word prayer: "My Lord and my God!" This exclamation reveals the heart of this famous doubter.

We need to recognize what Thomas did: that Jesus is the leader. "Following Jesus doesn't get us where we want to go. It gets us to where Jesus goes, where we meet him in resurrection surprise: 'My Lord and my God!'" (p. 242).

Between the comfortable corruption of the Caiaphas way and the ascetic elitism of the Essene way is the worshipfully obedient praying of Thomas on the Jesus way.

Key Adjectives

Caiaphas: privileged, exploitative, commodifying, oppressive, religious, threatened, professional, important, aristocratic, lavish, prominent, powerful, impatient, controlling, managing, self-serving, corrupt, ambitious, calculating, political, secularized, wealthy, Hellenized, influential, ambitious

Essenes: radical, sectarian, ascetic, outraged, pure, uncontaminated, strict, alternative, simple, focused, moral, exact, elite, unsympathetic, single-minded, trained, disciplined, austere, ordered, self-sufficient, scrupulous, careful, communal, fiery

Jesus: intimate, relational

Quotations to Consider

"A priest stands in the middle between us and God, between God and us. . . . The priest offers God to us, all of God, everything that God is and does — a gift to us. The priest offers us to God, everything that we are and do — a gift to God" (pp. 222-23).

"Sometimes priests, impatient with being servants of God and God's people, insist on taking control of the relationship, managing God's business and our salvation. When that happens we have the scandal of the bad priest" (p. 224).

"The widespread interest in what is often termed 'spirituality' is in some ways a result of disillusionment and frustration with institutional religion" (pp. 229-30).

"Being religious does not translate across the board into being good or trustworthy. Religion is one of the best covers for sin of almost all kinds" (p. 230).

"The devil does some of his best work behind stained glass" (p. 230).

"I don't think we are going to find much support in Jesus for the contemporary preference for the golf course as a place of worship over First Baptist Church" (p. 231).

"Synagogues and temples, cathedrals, chapels, and storefront meeting halls provide continuity in place and community for Jesus to work his will among his people. A place, a building, collects stories and develops associations that give local depth and breadth and continuity to our experience of following Jesus" (p. 231).

"Jesus prophesied judgment on the temple but he didn't boycott it. Jesus was not scrupulous about purity" (p. 239).

"Jesus obviously wasn't gathering followers from the moral and spiritual upper-class of society. Jesus wasn't recruiting tried and true, tested and proven fighters, highly disciplined troops for the eschatological warfare that was imminent" (p. 239).

"Most of us, at least at times, are mightily tempted by the Essene strategy. We want a church, an organization, that is committed and serious, that

has a well-thought-out strategy and a clear goal of where it is going —
like the Essenes" (p. 239).

"When we follow Jesus, it means that we don't know exactly what it
means, at least in detail" (p. 240).

"When Jesus says "Follow me" and we follow, we don't know where we
will go next or what we will do next. That is why we follow the one who
does know" (p. 240).

Questions for Interaction

1. Peterson says we all need a priest (someone to present God to us
   and us to God) because we're not good at meeting our God-need
   ourselves. Who serves as a priest for you? In what way?
2. Peterson says that there is no worship without sacrifice. What does
   he mean by this?
3. A sacrifice doesn't have to be much, but it must be the best we have
   to offer. Why is the quality of our sacrifices generally so low?
4. If prayer is a daily sacrifice of who we are to God, what are you offering to God in prayer: the best of yourself, or something less?
   How might a priest of some kind help you offer your best?
5. Has following Jesus made your life more comfortable or less comfortable? In what ways?
6. Institutional religion is easily corrupted. Have you been bitten by
   the anti-institutional church bug? If so, how has it affected your following of Jesus?
7. Peterson comments, "We sometimes say, thoughtlessly I think, that
   the church is not a building. It's people. I'm not so sure" (p. 231).
   What do you think of this observation?
8. If the building isn't the "church" per se, how does it operate as an
   important "member" of the church?
9. We are all drawn to the comfortable life on one side and the ascetic
   life on the other. Which one has the greater appeal for you, and
   why?
10. What is the attraction of detailed, proscriptive programs for spiritu-
    ality and church?

**Praying with traveling companions on the Jesus way:
H. E. Fosdick (1878-1969)**

Especially we pray you to make Christianity more Christian.

The Way of Josephus;
or, Avoiding the Detours of Selfishness and Violence

(pp. 243-71)

Summary

Josephus came onto the scene after Jesus was gone and while the early Christian community was forming. Even though he made sure he tried out all the religious options available to him at the time, he didn't give the unimpressive Jesus movement more than a glance. It wasn't up to snuff.

Zealots — those who wanted to get rid of Rome and were willing to use violence to do it — were crawling all over the scene during and after Jesus' lifetime. In fact, in some ways, Jesus looked like them. But the complete lack of violence that characterized his way on earth and what followed it prove that he was far from one. "The final and convincing proof that Jesus was not a Zealot was that after his crucifixion there was no revolt, no violence. No looting. No killing. Nothing" (p. 147).

Unlike the death-to-the-end Zealots, Josephus switched teams and joined the Romans when the tide went against the Jewish rebels. He then became the Jewish mouthpiece for the empire, appealing to the Jews who were besieged in Jerusalem and later writing books with this underlying message: "Don't be so Jewish. Be a Roman Jew. That's what it means to be a real Jew." Josephus was "the consummate opportunist" (p. 252). It was all about him.

The church of the crucified Jesus got its feet wet in a world of violence. The early leaders of the church were mocked and violently persecuted — arrested, imprisoned, killed. But they weren't intimidated. Resurrection filled their imaginations.

In an age when many Christians suffered violence, there is no record of Christians dealing out violence. The closest they came to it was on the night of Jesus' arrest before his crucifixion, when Peter cut off Malchus's ear. But Jesus told Peter to put away his sword, and that was that. It is interesting to note that faith in God is what fed the violence of the Zealots, and faith in God is also what snuffed it out of the followers of Jesus. What explains this? Peterson points out that Jesus' followers "were following the resurrected Jesus, and the Jesus who was now living in them wasn't killing anyone" (p. 255).

Charismatic leaders have often used warlike causes to exercise personal power, exploiting people's emotions and drugging their minds. Josephus was a master at that. He was able to take what was left of his former religious passion and harness it for his own benefit as a propaganda artist. "It was a bastard religion in the service of a cause" (p. 255). The cause: Josephus.

What Josephus had wasn't belief. Not really. The Zealots, on the other hand, were full of belief. Passionate about God, justice, and freedom, they went headlong after evil. But the war against evil becomes evil itself in violence.

But here's the good news: It is possible to retain "the energy and focus and zeal" (p. 261) of the Zealots without becoming violent or being intimidated by violence. The early Christians following the way of Jesus were neither violent nor cowed by violence. The key to their non-Zealot zeal, Peterson says, is found in one of those untranslatable words: *homothumadon.*

Homothumadon is usually translated as "of one accord" or "of one mind" or "together." But those translations are far too tame, according to Peterson. "*Homothumadon* has fire in it. It is the passion of a consensual, unanimous response to something God does. We don't work it up. It is always dependent on something God has just done, or is about to do, or we are participating in. . . . It is fire. And it marks the church as it is formed by the Holy Spirit" (pp. 262-63).

Not a "spiritual" word in itself, it is what best describes what happens to the church when the Spirit has his way with us. It flows from the same power of the Holy Spirit that raised Jesus from the dead and becomes alive and active in the followers of Jesus.

This is not something we can whip up for ourselves with a rousing talk or emotional singing. This is the work of God in us. We can't contrive it, but we can recognize it. The hard part is recognizing when other forms of *homothumadon* are fanned into flame around us, such as the patriotism that war fever brings.

While "there are no secrets to living out the Christian life," prayer is basic to it: "It never takes place without prayer" (p. 264). Prayer keeps us God-oriented and personal. It's not something we can put off until we develop "prayer skills." It's the context in which we live the Jesus life.

The life of God in us spills over in a fire that brings more life. A life-giving fire, not the death-dealing, violent fire of the Zealots, not the self-promoting, opportunistic fire of Josephus.

The presupposition of Josephus is "I rule." The presupposition of Zealots is "God doesn't rule, but he should, and we need to do what we can so that he does rule." Our presupposition is "God rules, I don't, and I don't need to be in charge or worry about it even though I get to be part of it." Confidence and humility come together. This leads not to passivity but to a freedom to participate in the kingdom of God — and praying is an essential part of participating.

Prayer keeps our kingdom work personal. Impersonal approaches lead to opportunism (using people to get them to do what we want them to do) and violence (dispensing with people who get in the way) instead of life.

Between the charismatic opportunism of the Josephus way and the violent revolution of the Zealot way is the humbly confident praying of the faithful community on the Jesus way.

Key Adjectives

Josephus: impressive, despicable, verbose, prominent, assured, obsessive, meticulous, religious, precocious, charismatic, cunning, strategic, intriguing, ingenious, masterful, brightest, best, brilliant, eloquent, quick, manipulating, talented, charming, opportunistic, conniving

Zealots: revolutionary, sectarian, violent, conspiring, anonymous, goading, provoking, furious, adamant, convicted, believing, committed, passionate, popular, heroic, glamorous, noble, admired, biblical, blind, immature

Jesus: personal, prayerful, intimate, familiar, unique, particular, humble, confident, relaxed, accepting

Quotations to Consider

"Religious propaganda is religion without morals, without truth (theology), without relationships — it is unadulterated *means*" (p. 255).

"There is to be no violence in the cause of God. None. End of discussion" (p. 259).

"When we believe that God is on our side, that we have a mission to perform sanctioned by God, it is easy to do anything that we think will be effective — using force, pushing, bullying, manipulating, and, yes, killing — to bring victory to God. It is virtually irresistible when the opposition is identified as Evil" (p. 259).

"There was something burning within those followers of Jesus, drawing them together in the same mind and spirit, something akin to the energy of anger, but without anger" (p. 262).

"Prayer is basic because it provides the primary language for everything that takes place on the way of Jesus" (p. 264).

"Prayer is not something added on to the Christian life. . . . It is the language in which that life is lived out, nurtured, developed, revealed, informed; the language in which it believes, loves, explores, seeks, and finds. There are no shortcuts or detours" (p. 264).

"We can only *pray* our lives into the way of following Jesus" (p. 265).

"Prayer both internalizes and embodies Jesus; there is no other way into the Way" (p. 265).

"Prayer is the way we get the following (not just the feeling!) inside us" (p. 265).

"The gospel was not something private that [the first generation of Christians] cultivated in the cozy security of their homes and hearts; it was public, the most powerful force in human history, shaping the destiny of nations as well as the souls of men and women" (p. 268).

"Following Jesus gets us little or nothing of what we commonly think we need or want or hope for. Following Jesus accomplishes nothing on the world's agenda. . . . Following Jesus has everything to do with this world, but almost nothing in common with this world" (p. 270).

"We are faced with this wonderful, or not-so-wonderful, irony: Jesus — most admired, most worshiped (kind of), most written about. And least followed" (p. 271).

Questions for Interaction

1. How can we make the most of opportunities without becoming opportunistic like Josephus?
2. In what ways might you be tempted to use Christianity to make things better for yourself?
3. How did the early Christians maintain their fire without getting caught up in the Zealots' way of violence? What can we learn from them?
4. Does *homothumadon* sound like something regularly experienced at your church stewardship committee meeting? If not, why not? What takes its place?
5. How have you experienced *homothumadon* in Christian community?
6. Peterson writes, "We can't put off prayer until we 'get good at it'" (p. 265). Do you feel good at it? Do you put it off? What's the problem with thinking about how we feel about it?
7. What makes prayer so essential to the communal fire of Christian *homothumadon*?
8. How can we develop humility — which means staying human and not developing god-pretensions — without becoming doormats?
9. How can we live confidently without becoming smug?
10. How can we participate in what God's doing in the world without trying to take over?

Praying with traveling companions on the Jesus way:
George E. L. Cotton (1813-1866)

O God, who made of one blood all nations to dwell on the face of the whole earth and who sent your blessed Son to preach peace to those who are far off and to those that are near, grant that all everywhere may seek after you and find you. Bring the nations into your fold, pour out your Spirit upon all flesh, and hasten your kingdom, through the same, your Son, Jesus Christ our Lord.